Helping your pupils
to work cooperatively

The Little Books of Life Skills

In our rapidly changing world, education is becoming less and less about imparting knowledge than it is about empowerment. We now want to make sure our children get the skills they need, not only to engage with and take responsibility for their own learning, but to successfully take part in a range of experiences throughout their lives.

The strategies and activities in the *Little Books of Life Skills* will help children see themselves as champions of their own world, a critical step in meeting the outcomes of the **Every Child Matters** agenda. Each title in the series will help children get the skills they need to enjoy and achieve – in school and beyond.

The five *Little Books of Life Skills* are:

- *Helping your pupils to ask questions*
- *Helping your pupils to be resilient*
- *Helping your pupils to communicate effectively and manage conflict*
- *Helping your pupils to think for themselves*
- *Helping your pupils to work cooperatively*

Helping your pupils
to work cooperatively

Kath Murdoch and Jeni Wilson

Routledge
Taylor & Francis Group

LONDON AND NEW YORK

First published by Curriculum Corporation 2004
PO Box 177
Carlton South Vic 3053
Australia

This edition published 2008 by Routledge
2 Park Square, Milton Park, Abingdon, Oxon, OX14 4RN, United Kingdom

Simultaneously published in the USA and Canada
by Routledge
270 Madison Ave, New York, NY 10016

Routledge is an imprint of the Taylor & Francis Group, an informa business

Illustrations by Aja Bongiorno
Typeset in Stone Serif by FiSH Books, Enfield, Middx.
Printed and bound in Great Britain by TJ International Ltd, Padstow, Cornwall

Dedication
To Holly, Gretta, Ethan and Madison, may they enjoy positive and cooperative
relationships.

Acknowledgements
We would like to thank all the teachers who have trialled our ideas or allowed us to
develop our ideas in their classroom or with them during professional development
programs. Special thanks go to teachers from: Ballan Primary, Kilmore Primary,
Hawthorn West Primary, Princes Hill Primary, Ringwood Heights Primary, Aberfeldie
Primary, Terang Secondary College and the Leongatha region. Examples are included
from the classrooms of: Kerri Friggi-Harrison, Jill Parker, Joanna Stanford and David
Stephens.

British Library Cataloguing in Publication Data
A catalogue record for this book is available from the British Library

Library of Congress Cataloging in Publication Data
A catalog record has been requested for this book

ISBN 10: 0-415-44731-3
ISBN 13: 978-0-415-44731-7

Contents

What is cooperative learning?

In simple terms, cooperative learning occurs when a group of pupils works together towards a shared goal. Cooperative learning is more than working alongside others – pupils can be working in groups with minimal interaction. When structured well, cooperative learning involves pupils in high-level interaction with others. They work as a team, sharing resources, ideas, feedback and a shared goal. This usually means a group product is completed.

What does cooperative learning look like?

The most obvious evidence of cooperative learning in a classroom is where arrangements are made for pupils to meet and work together in a variety of groupings. Tables are clustered together or larger tables are used around which several pupils may sit. In classrooms where cooperative learning is valued, pupils are usually seated in groups during most of the school day, making it easier for them to work cooperatively when required.

The most powerful evidence of cooperative learning is the ease with which pupils are able to work with others. There is a palpable collaborative atmosphere in a room where cooperative learning is the norm, where pupils are regularly expected to work with others and where the skills and processes needed to make it work are understood by all. Cooperative learning works best in classrooms where pupil-centred learning is valued by the teacher and pupils.

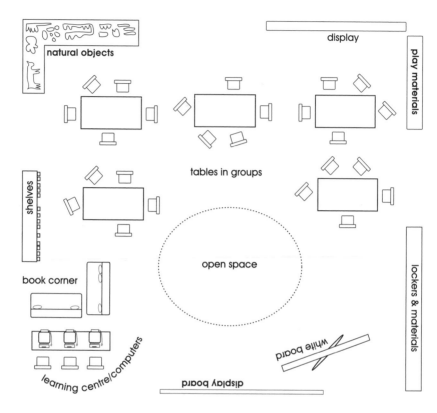

Features of cooperative learning

When cooperative learning is working effectively, the following features are
evident:

- Groups are working on a shared task (although individuals may be
  responsible for aspects of that task).

- Everyone in the group is aware of their roles and their responsibilities and
  there is a high level of individual accountability.

- Individuals feel valued and respected by the group and there is a high
  level of support and emotional safety in the classroom.

- Tasks in which groups are engaged are worthwhile – they are a
  meaningful component of the teaching and learning program.

- Pupils employ a range of skills such as communication (e.g. active listening), thinking (e.g. reflecting) and social skills (e.g. giving constructive feedback) as they work with others.
- Groups are formed in a range of ways for different purposes.
- Groups employ a range of targeted strategies (see page 31) to work towards their shared goal. Both teachers and pupils have a conscious repertoire of strategies they can use to help the process along.
- There are established and well understood protocols for how groups work together in the classroom. These protocols may be displayed and revisited on a regular basis.
- Pupils regularly reflect on the way they work as part of a cooperative group.
- Groups engage in cooperative and individual reflection on the way they work together.
- Cooperative skills are assessed by teachers and self-assessed by pupils.
- The products/outcomes of cooperative group work are assessed.
- Pupils experience cooperative group work across a range of learning areas: they may work on visual, mathematical, kinaesthetic, linguistic tasks, etc or combinations of these.
- Teachers and pupils value (through discussion, assessment, etc) both the processes they are using and the products they are working towards.

Cooperative learning is not:

- Pupils sitting at one table talking about their individual work.
- Sharing materials for individual work.
- Groups where only one or two pupils do all the work.

Cooperative learning is one variety of teaching approaches used in the classroom. It is not a total classroom program or oganisation strategy. It works best with other approaches.

Group Assessment

In my group there were

$\boxed{4}$ girls   and $\boxed{2}$ boys

- The <u>girls</u> did pay attention and listen.
- The <u>boys</u> did nothing and sat on their chairs.
- I like group work because <u>you have to work and you write</u>.
- The thing I don't like about group work is <u>Mark talks and doesn't listen</u>.

What are the benefits of cooperative learning?

The ability to work as part of a team is among the most vital things we can teach pupils at school. Cooperative skills are cited again and again by employers as highly desirable qualities of their employees, often prioritised over specific technical knowledge. There is little doubt that the skills associated with effective teamwork will continue to be vital to successful lifelong learning and active citizenship. Cooperative work provides a context in which pupils can develop important interpersonal skills for effective social interaction. Working closely with others (not just alongside them) teaches pupils to be more sensitive to difference, learn to compromise, share and communicate in a range of ways. In short, cooperative learning helps build pupils' capacity for healthy relationships with others as well as enhancing their learning outcomes. Cooperative learning can help build a safe and supportive environment in the classroom. This, in turn, provides a more positive context for pupils to learn. All classrooms include pupils whose learning styles favour social, interactive approaches. Opportunities to work cooperatively allow these pupils to work in their most preferred mode and allow all pupils to develop important life skills.

Cooperative learning is one of a variety of teaching approaches used in the classroom. It is not a total classroom program or organisation strategy and works best if combined with other approaches.

What do you like about working in groups?

I like how we sit in a circle first and sometimes I like how we make decisions about who's going to do what. Sometimes I don't like it how we make decisions because everybody might want to do the same thing, like if we have to cut up.

(Year 3 pupil)

What happens if everyone wants the same job?

I ask them: Do you want to do this? And I tell the rest there are other things to do. We all decide what we want to do and share the jobs. If everyone still wants to do the same job, I make it fair and think of something else I can do.

(Year 1 pupil)

For the pupil

The classroom may be one of the few places where pupils are regularly required to share, wait, take turns, compromise and accept criticism, and where they engage in meaningful, sustained dialogue with others. It is vital that we apprentice young people into 'the thinking, the talking and the doing' associated with true collaboration from the moment they enter school. Schools themselves – and many contexts beyond schools – require pupils to participate in discourses consistent with cooperating and working with others. Establishing relationships with and between pupils is at the very heart of effective teaching and learning. By regularly engaging pupils in cooperative activities, we can build those relationships and the skills that accompany their efficacy.

What have I learnt?

I learnt that you should always be a good listener. Because the people you are talking to can make you feel silly, angry, unhappy and lots more.

(Year 3 pupil)

What have I learnt?

I learnt that not listening to someone is not very nice. The people who were talking were hurt. I could tell by their faces.

(Year 3 pupil)

Un-cooperative class　　　　　　**Cooperative class**

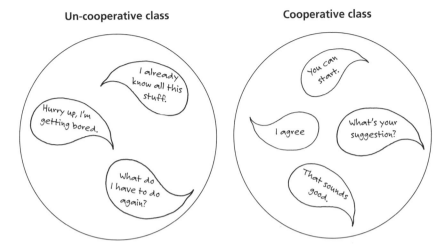

For the teacher

When pupils are working with each other, teachers can be 'freed up' to observe and assess pupils and to 'step in' at the point of need. Watching the way pupils interact with each other can provide powerful assessment data that is otherwise unavailable when pupils work individually or when the majority of teaching is directed to the whole class.

The benefits of cooperative learning have been identified and documented throughout the past twenty years (for example, Johnson & Johnson, 1987; Slavin, 1991). Many useful and lifelong skills can be enhanced, such as those listed below.

- Accepting and providing constructive criticism
- Active listening
- Questioning
- Checking and confirming
- Compromising
- Establishing agreed rules
- Following directions
- Goal setting

- Justifying viewpoints
- Linking ideas
- Maintaining focus/keeping on task
- Managing conflict or disagreement
- Managing time
- Negotiating
- Organising
- Planning
- Presenting ideas to others
- Problem solving
- Reflecting on learning, behaviour and thinking
- Reporting to others
- Risk taking
- Seeking clarification
- Self-assessment
- Sharing
- Suggesting alternatives
- Supporting or helping others
- Taking responsibility
- Teaching others
- Time management
- Understanding other points of view
- Using eye contact and appropriate body language.

The role of the teacher

The role of the teacher is critical to the success of cooperative learning in the classroom. The skills required for cooperative learning need to be explicitly taught to pupils of all ages and continually reinforced. From curriculum planning through to the physical layout of the classroom, the teacher's role is the key to success. Teachers that use cooperative learning in their classroom play multiple roles. The way these roles are enacted depends on the age group, the nature of the tasks pupils are engaged in, prior experiences of the pupils, and the broader school and community culture. The following roles form the basis of the teacher's repertoire in cooperative learning activities:

1. Explicit instruction
2. Modelling
3. Feedback
4. Intervention
5. Strategic task selection

1. Explicit instruction

Attempts to engage pupils in cooperative learning can be frustrating or less effective because we assume that pupils will know and be able to use the necessary skills. Even experienced adult learners can find cooperative group work challenging if they do not consciously consider the skills and protocols necessary for success. Thus, one of the most important roles of a teacher is to teach pupils about effective cooperation and conflict resolution. We believe there are four key understandings pupils need to develop. These are listed below, together with some suggestions for how to work towards these understandings.

Pupils need to understand that:

1. Cooperative learning benefits us in many ways, both at school and in life outside school.
2. Effective cooperation takes work. Teams can work effectively or ineffectively. There are ways of recognising an effective team.
3. We can influence the success of our team by the way we behave as individuals.
4. Everyone can learn to improve their capacity to cooperate with others.

Introductory activities

The activities suggested below provide some ideas for helping pupils develop these understandings.

- Pupils brainstorm their responses to the question: 'Why should we learn to work well in groups?' Use a strategy such as *Think–Pair–Share* (page 35).

- Pupils research job advertisements for a range of occupations and identify the skills and qualities required. Note that many positions explicitly state the need for people to be able to work as a team.

- Pupils talk to their parents/carers about the issue of cooperation. Pupils can ask their parents about situations when they are required to work as part of a team in their own working life.

- Invite a guest speaker to talk to pupils about the value of cooperative behaviour. For example, the school principal or a sports person. Being able to work as part of a team is critical to many situations and helps pupils see beyond the classroom context.

- Use the *Cooperative Quiz* statements (page 62) to stimulate discussion about cooperative group work.

- Pupils start a task and then work with a partner to complete it. Discuss why this was helpful and/or challenging.

- Create posters or charts to display in the classroom that answer the question: 'Why learn to cooperate?' (See other examples opposite.)

Why it's good to work in groups

- It's not hard
- You get more done
- You might not be able to do it otherwise
- Saves time
- You can help each other
- It's fun
- You get extras
- You can rest a bit sometimes

Things we do and say in groups

- Sharing
- Helping each other
- Taking turns
- Sharing ideas
- Listening
- Using quiet voices
- Encouraging each other
- Respecting ideas and people
- Being kind and appreciative

A good talker

- Speaks up
- Makes it interesting
- Looks at his/her partner
- Makes sure the listener understands
- Asks questions
- Doesn't walk away or look away
- Doesn't change the subject
- Doesn't fiddle
- Repeats if not understood
- Uses face/hands
- Changes voices

■ Consider the roles and responsibilities in a club or within a family. Are there rules and regulations that assist in the running of the household?

Y charts

It is important that we spend time teaching pupils what makes teams succeed or fail. One way of doing this is to create a Y chart with pupils about the qualities of effective teams and team members.

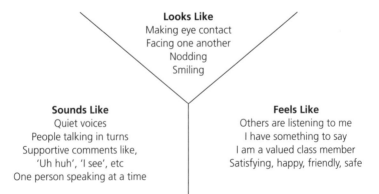

Looks Like
Making eye contact
Facing one another
Nodding
Smiling

Sounds Like
Quiet voices
People talking in turns
Supportive comments like,
'Uh huh', 'I see', etc
One person speaking at a time

Feels Like
Others are listening to me
I have something to say
I am a valued class member
Satisfying, happy, friendly, safe

Pupils complete the Cooperative Quiz (p 62) in small groups, and use their responses to discuss what a cooperative group is and isn't.

A similar, more detailed approach to defining the elements of effective group work can be to create a list of criteria for effective group interaction. By creating this list together, pupils develop a better understanding of what it means to work cooperatively, as well as having explicit guidelines for reflection, peer and self-assessment.

Fishbowl strategy

Another way to teach pupils about what makes teams work is to use the fishbowl strategy. Here, one group engages in the given task while other pupils (maybe another group or the whole class) observe the processes they use. Fishbowling works best when the observers are given a specific focus or question to guide their observations, for example: 'As you watch the group work together, I want you to make a note of the things that help keep the group focused and on task'.

Fishbowl strategy
(students viewed
from above)

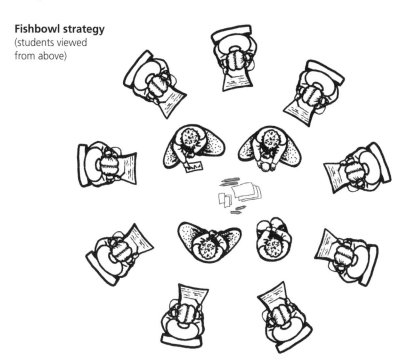

2. Modelling

If teachers expect pupils to work cooperatively, then they must practise what they teach! One powerful way to help pupils learn to cooperate is to see regular, effective models of cooperation around them. It is often said that pupils learn more from what teachers do than what they say. Pupils need to see that the teacher also contributes as part of various teams.

Team teaching is one very obvious way of modelling cooperation. Even when this is not the normal structure in the school, try to team teach at least some of the time – it's a great way to model (and practise!) working with others. Tell pupils that you plan and reflect with others, let them hear teachers making collective decisions, and the way they communicate, question, reflect and plan.

Teachers' dealings with parents and the wider school community all provide opportunities to model collaboration. Interactions with pupils themselves on a daily basis provide a chance to model cooperation and the language and behaviours associated with it. Invite pupils to help make decisions, solve problems and set class goals.

3. Feedback

Once pupils are organised to work cooperatively, it is vital that they receive constructive and ongoing feedback from their teachers as well as from each other. Giving and modelling feedback is an important role of the teacher. Regular and constructive feedback helps keep pupils mindful of what is expected, promotes accountability, helps develop skills and enables pupils to set individual and group goals. It provides a rehearsal for their own reflections on their role and group work.

Feedback can also act as a reminder or prompt to all – it serves as instruction. In order to provide effective and transferable feedback, teachers need to:

- be clear about what is expected of pupils as they work
- allow time during and at the end of the session to give pupils feedback
- provide both individual and group feedback
- focus both on what is working well and on what needs improving.

Feedback can be provided on both what the pupils are working on and how they are working. It may be written or oral, public or private, formal or informal. Some suggestions for managing and providing quality feedback are as follows:

- Identify certain skills/behaviours that will be observed during a session and let pupils know they will receive feedback on that.

> As you work, I am going to observe and give feedback on the body language you are using in your group. What do you think I will be looking for?

- Make a deliberate effort to acknowledge the efforts made by individuals. The *Thank You Slips* (pages 54–55) can be used for this purpose. A little note of encouragement given to a pupil goes a long way to enhancing their confidence and motivation. Be specific about what you are thanking them for.

> Thank you for waiting for your turn.

- Show pupils anecdotal notes or checklists you are keeping as you watch them work cooperatively.
- Give constructive feedback on pupil and teacher goals.
- To provide detailed feedback, focus on one group intensively rather than trying to observe all pupils in the room.

✔ Staying on task
✔ Focused
✔ Using quiet voices

Pupils need to know when the behaviour/attitude/language they are using is getting in the way of the group's progress. One of the most important aspects of the feedback role is to help pupils see what they do/say and how it impacts on the group. Some pupils need to be actually 'shown' what they do and can do. We have seen some powerful teaching occur when teachers respectfully mirror a pupil's actions back to them, and then ask them to think about how that could be changed or modified to help the group work more effectively. This can be counterproductive if pupils are embarrassed, so this needs to be done sensitively.

> Team Terrific!
> Jayden got onto task quickly and stayed on task. The whole team listened to each other's ideas today.

4. Intervention

Closely related to the role of providing feedback is the role of 'intervention'; of working with the groups at strategic moments. Our key goal is for pupils to be able to work cooperatively with minimal assistance from the teacher. To get to this point, however, many groups and individual pupils require deliberate and focused instruction as they are working. Observation is vital and pupils should be allowed some time to work through problems or issues as they arise. But when those problems block the progress of the group, it may be time to 'step in and teach'. In addition, pupils with special needs may need additional support or instruction to be able to effectively work with others in the group.

Typical contexts for intervention include:

- Persistent off-task behaviour by one or more group members
- A noise level or behaviour that is distracting or disruptive to others
- One or more pupils clearly not participating in the group
- Sustained arguments or conflict
- A misunderstanding of the task.

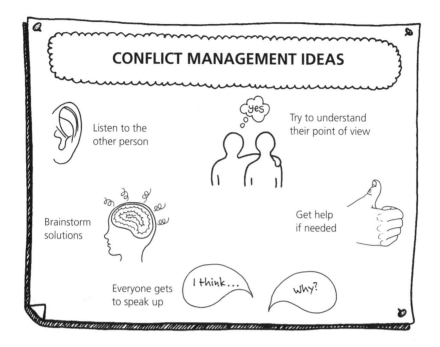

Sample strategies for successful intervention

■ Join the group for a while and offer suggestions/questions as an additional group member.

■ Rather than singling out the group in front of the class, sit with them and help them deal with the problem.

■ Sit alongside individuals experiencing difficulties and 'coach' them in what to say or do next.

■ Ask the group to restate their understanding of the task and what they intend to do next.

■ Invite individuals or groups to observe other more successful groups for a short period and then report back to their own group on strategies they could try.

■ Direct the group back to posters/charts around the room showing skills/behaviours and protocol.

Pupils need to know that you expect them to work cooperatively and that you will intervene to assist them towards that – a malfunctioning group cannot be excused from the task. General reflection time at the end of the session can be used to discuss effective and not so effective cooperative group strategies.

5. Strategic task selection

Perhaps one of the most obvious but least identified roles of the teacher in cooperative learning is to plan worthwhile, rich tasks for pupils to cooperatively engage in. Some tasks do not lend themselves to cooperative learning or may not involve pupils in learning something worthwhile.

Tasks that suit cooperative learning:

Are generally open ended

Tasks that are open ended immediately require discussion, problem solving, decision making and often encourage creativity. Closed tasks that have only one answer or outcome can set up unnecessary conflict or, more commonly, require little actual cooperation. Examples of open ended tasks include:

- Creating a model to illustrate a shared understanding about a topic
- Designing an experiment to test a particular theory/hypothesis
- Creating a short role-play or scenario to perform to others
- Brainstorming and bundling words or statements about a topic.

Are linked to a current shared inquiry or topic that, in itself, deals with worthwhile and meaningful concepts

Engagement in a cooperative task is enhanced when all pupils have some investment in the content they are working on. When the group has ownership of, or are emotionally engaged in, the task they are more likely to contribute to it. Some examples of such tasks include:

- As part of a unit of work on Britishness, the pupils discuss and record what they know about a topic such as traditional British cultures. As a group, they code the list of understandings to show ideas with which they all agree and those they are less sure of.

- At the end of a unit of work such as shelters and structures, young pupils cooperatively design the ideal play house that could be erected in the playground.
- As a part of a unit on persuasive writing, older pupils work cooperatively to generate a list of criteria to be used to assess their final written pieces.

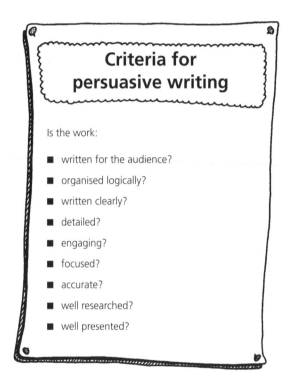

Criteria for persuasive writing

Is the work:

- written for the audience?
- organised logically?
- written clearly?
- detailed?
- engaging?
- focused?
- accurate?
- well researched?
- well presented?

Organising the classroom

Classroom set up

We have seen cooperative learning happening successfully in a wide range of classrooms. An essential ingredient for success is an informed and committed teacher – if the classroom has one of these then anything is possible! There is no doubt, however, that cooperative learning runs more smoothly when the physical environment supports it. Provide pupils with a defined area in which to work, for example, sitting around a table, a circle of chairs or cushions, or gathered around an object or text with which they will work.

The layout of tables and chairs in the room is important. If tables are routinely grouped in clusters, it is easier for pupils to work in small groups. The way pupils are seated can have a real impact on how well the group works. While there should be a place in the room that pupils can return to as their 'space', establish the understanding that they will not always work there. They need to be comfortable working in various places around the room.

Floor space should be available if possible, especially when there are materials that need sorting or spreading out. Keep an area of the classroom aside for quiet or individual work, use room dividers or corralled areas for this purpose. Flexibility is the key to supporting collaboration through physical spaces. Even very small classrooms can have pupils working in groups. In fact, grouping tables/desks usually provides more room to move. We have observed that classrooms with a minimum of clutter (and this may mean reducing the amount of materials/work on display) tend to foster a more calm and focused working atmosphere. Table and chair arrangements should encourage pupils to face each other. A circle shape is ideal as it directs everyone to the shared space and allows eye contact across the group.

Establish roles and responsibilities

One of the most useful organisation techniques for effective cooperative learning is to teach pupils about the various roles that individuals can play in groups. These roles can be allocated for various activities, although we would caution teachers against using them all the time. They are primarily used to identify the different roles in group tasks.

Roles help pupils build their capacity to use a wide range of skills and promote individual accountability. Examples of some of these roles include:

- **Problem solver** (makes suggestions on how to sort out a problem if it arises)
- **Recorder** (records the group's ideas)
- **Reporter** (reports back to the class, teacher or another group)
- **Time keeper** (keeps an eye on the clock and lets the group know how much time they have)
- **'Go-for'** (gathers and returns necessary materials)
- **Encourager** (makes a point of ensuring that good ideas are acknowledged and that people are involved)
- **Observer** (watches and listens to the group, identifying how they are working together, their strengths and weaknesses and then reports back to them or the class)
- **Organiser/coordinator** (gets the group going and keeps them on track)

Naturally, while the roles are helpful for many activities, there are times when their use is unnecessary or when they need not be explicitly allocated. Sometimes, individuals can become so fixated on their roles, they lose sight of the tasks at hand. Display posters around the room that remind pupils of the features of each role. It is also useful to make role cards/badges/labels that can be worn by pupils during cooperative learning tasks (see page 59 for examples).

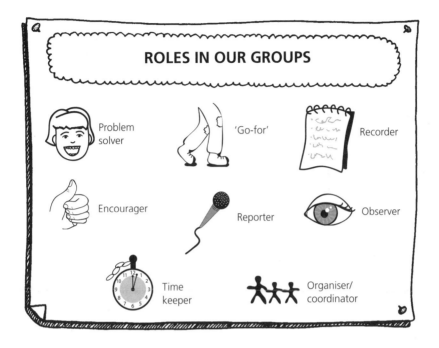

Foster individual accountability

When cooperative learning is effective, every pupil in the group is accountable for their contribution to the group task. They are responsible for their own learning and also understand that they are there to support and contribute to the work of the group. In cooperative learning, every member of the group drives the task; there are no passengers.

Some of the methods we have found useful for fostering individual accountability include:

- Assigning roles
- Giving individual pupils preparation time prior to joining the group, ensuring they are ready to contribute (see *From Me to We*, p 63)
- Asking individuals to reflect on their contributions and devise goals for continual improvement (see assessment ideas, p 43)

- Ensuring that seating arrangements promote face to face interaction
- Encouraging the sharing of materials and tasks. For example, when brainstorming a topic, each pupil takes it in turn to record ideas
- Teaching pupils to make a plan of how they will complete a task and who will do what
- Setting individual and group goals
- Making time for assessment, including self, group and peer (see *Imagine You Are the Teacher*, p 64)
- Incorporating reflection time into lessons.

Establish clear protocol

An important organisational element behind effective cooperative learning is an agreed understanding of 'how we work together in groups'. It is important to develop this protocol with pupils, to display it clearly and to reinforce it regularly. Guidelines for group work are even more powerful when they extend beyond the individual classroom and are shared by the school as a whole, or by a team of teachers.

When working in a group, we each agree to:

Participate in the task
Listen respectfully to others
Take turns
Help others
Try to solve problems
Use positive and encouraging language
Show our interest and enthusiasm.

Types of groupings

There are many different ways of grouping pupils for cooperative learning. Different kinds of groups serve different purposes. Some examples of pupil groupings include:

- Teacher selected
- Pupil selected
- Long-term 'base' groups (groups that work with each other regularly or for an ongoing project)
- Short-term groups (per activity/task).

The size of the group is primarily determined by the purpose and nature of the task. Working in pairs is often a first step in learning to be cooperative and the size of the group will increase as pupils become more skilled. We find that when groups exceed four or five pupils, it can be more difficult for them to function effectively.

The classroom program should allow for pupils to work in a range of grouping types and sizes, as well as working on their own or as part of the whole class.

Grouping strategies and arrangements

Throughout the day or during the course of a lesson, pupils can be grouped informally to discuss a problem, complete a short task, share work or provide feedback. Informal groups are usually quite random in nature – pupils can end up working with anyone. It is important that pupils are grouped randomly some of the time as they need the experience of working with a wide range of people. There are countless techniques and tactics for random grouping. Some suggestions follow.

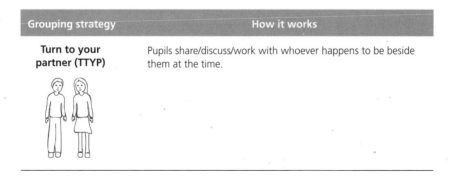

Grouping strategy	How it works
Turn to your partner (TTYP)	Pupils share/discuss/work with whoever happens to be beside them at the time.

Grouping strategy	How it works

Number off

Pupils are 'numbered off' according to the group size/number of groups required. All the pupils with the same number form a group.

Line ups/count offs

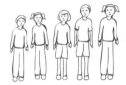

Pupils line up in order, using a given criteria. For example: house numbers, height, exact ages (to the day!). The line is then segmented into groups.

Match ups

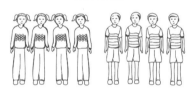

Pupils find other people who share a given criteria. For example: eye or hair colour, birthday month, number of family members, colour of clothing.

Group cards

Pupils are given cards/stickers with particular words, symbols, etc on them. They need to find the matching cards. This strategy can be tied to the current topic.

- Matching up letters to form a key word or words to form a sentence.
- Linking paragraphs from the same text.
- Matching up question and answer.
- Linking parts of a mathematical equation.

Grouping strategy	How it works

Round the clock

Pupils are each given (or they draw) a clock face. They organise a partner for each of the 12 hours on the clock. Teachers can then ask them to, for example, 'work with your 2 o'clock partner'.

Jigsaw pieces

Individual pupils are given a piece of puzzle or picture. They must then find the other people who hold the remaining puzzle pieces. These can be linked to the topic of study.

Lucky dip

Fill a bag or box with a collection of objects that can be grouped, such as coloured buttons, counters or blocks. Pupils select them 'lucky dip' style and then form groups with others holding the same kind of object.

String partners

The teacher or a pupil holds a pile of lengths of string in their hand (held in the centre so that both ends of the string can be picked up by pupils). The number of string lengths should be equal to half the class. So, if you have 28 pupils, you have 14 lengths. Ask pupils to take hold of one end of a piece of string. Then release the pile and pupils work out who is holding the other end! This becomes their partner. If there is an odd number of pupils, two pupils may select the same end, forming one group of three.

Mixed groups

Mixed groups refer to ability, gender, age, learning styles, etc. When teachers deliberately construct mixed groups, they help ensure that pupils work with a wide range of people. Pupils can also benefit from the modelling shown by others and from diverse points of view. Random grouping does not always result in equitable and diverse groups; teachers may need to deliberately construct groups to ensure this is the case for certain tasks.

Shared needs/interests

Sometimes, groups can be formed around shared needs or interests. For example, a shared need to work on particular writing skills. In this context, a cooperative task may be designed specifically for those pupils. Within a unit of work, some pupils may identify a similar question for investigation and may work in a group accordingly.

Friendship/pupil-selected groups

Pupils should be given opportunities to work with their choice of team mates. There are some contexts in which working with others with whom we have trusting relationships helps us get the job done more efficiently and satisfyingly. When given the opportunity to experience self-selected groups, pupils quickly realise that the friends they like to play with are not always the people that they learn best with.

Dealing with challenging behaviours

Sensitivity to individuals is essential when grouping. The following strategies may assist with specific challenges.

The dominant pupil

- Skill development sessions, particularly listening, are beneficial.
- Ask them to be the silent observer.
- If this behaviour stifles other group members' participation, try grouping dominant pupils together.
- Use 'talk tokens' to ensure equal participation.

The quiet/reluctant pupil

- Positively reinforce participation.
- Pair or re-group with other quiet/like pupils.
- Involve in non-threatening activities that highlight their strengths.
- Have pupils set their own achievable goals.
- Allocate specific roles in which they can achieve success.
- When ready, have them share with small groups at first.

The disinterested pupil

- Capitalise on areas of interest to that pupil.
- Have clear expectations and group member roles.
- Allocate small tasks.
- Create opportunities for them to make choices.

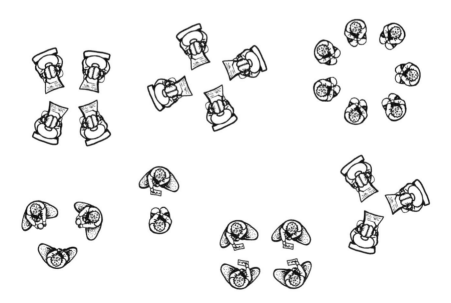

The disruptive pupil

- Give the pupil responsibilities they can handle.
- Praise all cooperative behaviour.
- Ask them to be the silent observer/peer assessor.
- If this continually affects the groups operation, introduce an individual or paired project.

It is worth remembering that these pupils want to 'fit in', possibly more than others. In very rare cases it will be appropriate to exclude pupils from cooperative group activities. Isolation should not become a regular event but teachers are in the best position to judge whether this is appropriate. Violent behaviour, for instance, may result in exclusion from cooperative group work. Wherever possible support pupils to join in activities.

Strategies and activities

5

There are a wide variety of strategies and structures that can be used to support cooperative learning in the classroom. Several examples are provided here. We have found it useful to teach pupils the names and purposes of the different strategies so they can be referred to across subjects/classes and quickly employed.

Jigsaw

The jigsaw grouping strategy is an excellent way to encourage all pupils to participate in and to contribute to each other's learning by sharing their expert knowledge. It can also help pupils work through a larger volume of information in a shorter amount of time than if they were working alone.

- Begin by organising pupils into groups (usually of four to five). This is the home group.

- Each pupil in the group is responsible for gathering information from a particular source or answering a particular question. These become the experts and work with others in an expert group.

- Once the expert groups have completed their task, individuals return to their home group to share their new expertise.

Home group

Expert groups

Experts return to home group

☐ Home groups
■ Expert groups

Bundling

This strategy is a useful way to build cooperative skills at the same time as synthesising ideas.

- Individuals list/brainstorm ideas (words/questions/statements) in response to a key question or challenge. They record their ideas on cards or post-it notes/cards.

- Pupils then meet in groups to share their ideas. They organise the notes/cards into bundles that identify the same or similar ideas.

- As a group, pupils then decide on labels for each bundle and share these with the class. Ideas can then be further bundled and labelled.

What helps a group work well together?

Brainstorm:
- taking turns
- sharing
- being kind
- listening
- sitting around a table
- speaking clearly
- eye contact
- having all the equipment needed

Materials	**Behaviour**	**Communication**
• sharing • sitting around a table • having all the equipment needed	• not being silly • being kind • taking turns	• speaking clearly • listening • eye contact

Placemat

This strategy, devised by Barrie Bennett (2001), is an excellent way to foster equal involvement and sharing of materials. It involves pupils recording their ideas on a shared piece of paper: the 'placemat'.

- Divide a piece of paper (at least A3 size or bigger) into segments; one for each member of the group, with a central square or circle in the middle.

Why are some animals under threat of extinction?

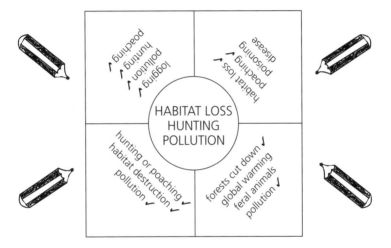

- Each pupil has a pen/pencil. The paper is placed in the middle of the table so that individuals can access their section easily. Provide the pupils with their task/question.

For example: for a unit of work on endangered species, ask them to brainstorm what they each know about the causes of endangerment. To solve a particular problem in the class/playground, each person begins by writing down a list of possible solutions. After watching a video or hearing a story, pupils write their ideas/reactions in their section of the placemat.

- Once individual ideas have been documented, the group shares.

- Each pupil takes a turn to read something from their list. Others tally or check off their own. Those ideas that have come up repeatedly are written in the central box.

- The group then devises a summary statement, conclusion or recommendation.

- Alternatively, the placemat is 'swivelled' around the group – either silently or with discussion. Each team member reads the others' contribution in turn.

- After ideas are shared, the central box is used for creating a group reflection statement.

- The central boxes can be cut out of the placemat and compared and contrasted with those from other groups.

Hot potato: cumulative brainstorm

Divide the class into groups. Each group is given a key question or focus for a brainstorm and a large sheet of paper. Groups are given a time frame in which to respond to the question. They are then asked to move around to the next group, read through their work and add to it. The activity is repeated until pupils return to their original sheet of paper and read through what others have added before reporting to the whole group.

Collaborative quiz

The emphasis in this activity is on coming to an agreed answer to a question as a team. Devise a set of simple, closed questions related to the current topic. They may be true or false type questions or those that require a simple, factual answer. For example: How many body parts does an insect have? Pupils are organised into teams. Read out the questions and have each team record their agreed answers. Teams can then swap their record sheets and check each others' work.

Think-Pair-Share

This strategy asks pupils to first think on their own (and note ideas if needed), then share with a friend (and look for patterns or similarities), and then with the whole class or group.

Prioritise

When you are working with items that can be listed, have the group work out how the items can be placed from most to least important. Teams should agree on their choices.

Silent jigsaw

This activity works well with pairs or trios. Use photos or pictures related to the topic. Cut each one up into pieces (not too many!). If working in pairs, mix the pieces of two jigsaws and divide the pile between each child. Pupils work together in silence to recreate each other's completed puzzle.

Build it one-at-a-time

Each pupil is given an equal number of construction components. They must take it in turns to add one component to a model, gradually creating something. The teams that are the most effective are those who use good communication skills.

Talk tokens

This is a good strategy for ensuring that discussions involve people more equally. Give each pupil in the group two to three counters. These are 'talk tokens'. Each pupil puts one token into a bowl in the centre of the circle whenever they speak; even if just agreeing with another comment. They should aim to 'spend' their tokens but once they have been spent they cannot say anything else.

Paired interviews/knee-to-knee and eye-to-eye

Pupils interview a partner about something and then report back to the group on what they found out. Ask them to sit facing each other directly.

Draw together

Have pupils work in pairs or threes to create a drawing/diagram. Explain that it is to be one picture planned and created by the team. The same strategy can be applied to making a model or using playdough.

Frequently asked questions (and trouble-shooting)

How many pupils should be in a group?

This depends mainly on the purpose of the activity. Other considerations include pupils' cooperative group experiences and skills, the age of the pupil, resources and the number of roles required for the task. Older pupils are generally better at working in larger groups (for example, four to six pupils), but cooperative group work can be counterproductive if not everyone can contribute to the task. Paired activities are suitable for pupils of all ages.

How can you assess individual contributions?

Where individual contributions need to be assessed, individual tasks may be more suitable. However, the work of individuals can be assessed within cooperative group work by the following methods:

- For written work, each pupil writes in a different coloured pen
- Group work is recorded (audio or video) for later review
- Teachers use an observation schedule to focus on what needs to be assessed
- Self-, peer or group assessment

Chris	Slow starter but got heaps done in the end. Great team member and individual worker.
Helen	Started very slow but got the rhythm towards the end. She is an average team worker and an average individual worker.
Anna	Went well all the 5 weeks. Great worker – team and individual.
Tom	Tom is a great worker. Started and ended well. Got a lot of work done.

Should cooperative skills be taught in isolation?

Cooperative skills are easily taught within everyday classroom routines, however where explicit attention to particular skills is required, a task may be designed to demonstrate or practise the skills. This task should be purposefully simple so that pupils can focus on the skills required. Simulated recall (where pupils review video recordings of their group actions) can be valuable for reflecting on and discussing specific skills.

Roles can be used to highlight the range of interdependent jobs and skills to be performed by group members. If roles are used, the teacher might allocate these to ensure that all pupils have a chance to perform a range of roles. If roles are always pupil selected, they may not choose certain roles and therefore not develop particular skills, for example, confident and assertive speaking.

What sort of changes will be required to my classroom set up to facilitate cooperative group work?

Tables rather than desks are more conducive to team work. These should be small enough for pupils to be able to hear and see all others in the team. They should be large enough to accommodate shared work such as poster-sized paper. Space on the floor for groups is also useful. Other changes needed to create a supportive classroom environment may be necessary so that pupils learn to value team work and others' contributions.

How can you get all pupils to do their fair share?

When cooperative groups work well all team members are accountable for their individual contribution to the group product and process. Each team member also has the responsibility to encourage and support other team members. The following ideas could be used to encourage all pupils to do their fair share.

- Tag and use roles within groups.
- Structure feedback so that individual accountability is the focus.
- Use self- and group assessment to highlight such issues as individual accountability.
- Brainstorm class lists of what great teams do.
- Consider giving shared assessment results, that is, everyone in the team receives the same final assessment.

What if pupils don't want to work in groups?

Most pupils do enjoy working with others but may lack the skills to do so. Sometimes pupils think that they can do better when working alone. In other words they do not recognise the value of team work. Skill development and reinforcing the importance and usefulness of being a good team member may be necessary. In some cases pupils can choose whether or not to work with others; while at other times this may not be negotiable. Be very explicit about the reasons for team work and give positive feedback to those who do work well as a team.

Explicit teaching of the skills needed for effective cooperation can help pupils who are reluctant to participate. Ask: What do you need to learn more about to help you to work well in a group? Mini lessons with small groups on eye contact, active listening, using talk tokens, asserting opinions, body language, etc can help equip pupils to work more successfully with others.

Reluctant pupils will also benefit from opportunities to choose the task or someone to work with as they are building their skills.

Importantly, remind pupils that working in a team is not an option – it is an expected skill in the classroom and beyond.

Tips for the teacher

- Practise! Cooperation skill development takes time and practice.
- Teach cooperative skills explicitly. Focus on how to listen, take turns and make decisions.
- Persistence, together with explicit teaching, worthy tasks and constructive feedback pays off.
- Be a good role model. For example, use names and encourage a range of opinions.
- Recognise and capitalise on individual strengths.
- Think about the physical set up of the classroom. Does it facilitate or hinder cooperation?
- Allow sufficient time. Because cooperative group work is so rich and requires multiple skill use, it can take more time for pupils to achieve desired outcomes.
- Vary group membership. The aim is for pupils to work in many different teams.
- Make a habit of reflecting regularly. This is useful for both pupils and teachers.
- Discuss, don't avoid conflict. Conflict can be seen as an opportunity to learn, but conflict management strategies are necessary.
- Give feedback about cooperative efforts as part of cooperative learning activities.
- Include assessment as part of the routine during cooperative tasks.
- Demonstrate that you value team work by working cooperatively with other teachers in the school.

8 Assessment and record keeping

The purpose of assessing pupils' cooperative work is to help teachers and pupils make decisions about their future learning experiences and to monitor progress. The methods that you choose are likely to be informal and should be purposeful, hence, reflection ideas are included in this section. Where possible, assessment should involve pupils.

Self-, peer and group assessment

When pupils are given regular opportunities for reflection on cooperative learning, they are better able to set goals and improve outcomes. This reflection can be carried out in a variety of ways by individuals or as a cooperative exercise in itself. These forms of assessment could be conducted orally, visually, as written text or performance based. They may utilise technology, for example, self- and group assessments may be included as part of a portfolio.

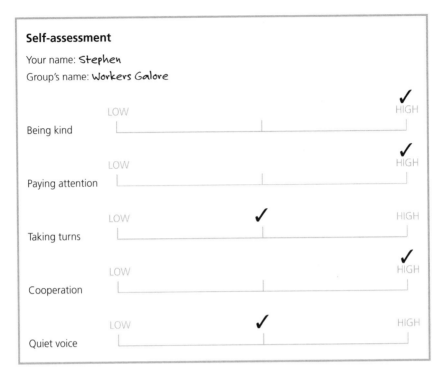

Self-assessment

Your name: Stephen

Group's name: Workers Galore

The following ideas could be adapted for different grade levels and a range of activities and purposes.

- Make time to complete self-assessment proformas at the end of sessions, where individuals and groups rate their own behaviour.
- Involve pupils in physical self-/peer/group assessment activities. For example:

  a) Pupils stand at a point along the continuum to signify their own (or groups') performance in response to a question, such as 'How well did you take turns?'

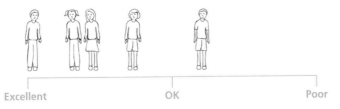

b) Pupils stand up in response to a question, such as 'Stand up if you used a quiet voice today'.

(NB Continuum and ranking exercises can also be done on paper.)

- Pupils either verbalise or record something positive that another group member did while working together. Provide sentence starters if necessary, for example:

> I was interested in the way you ...
> Thank you for ...
> Our group worked well because you ...

- Set up a panel of peer assessors to design criteria for observation of group work. They can present their findings to the group and/or whole class at the end of the session. To avoid embarrassment, peer assessors should be carefully briefed about what constitutes appropriate, constructive feedback.

- Reflections from journals and other writing can be used to document feelings, beliefs and attitudes towards cooperative group work. They can reveal very surprising information.

Tuesday

I think my behaviour is ...

I'll say 6 out of 10. I'm not saying 10 out of 10 because I think I talk too much on the floor. I'll try my hardest not to talk. You can't really help it but I'll just try anyway.

Helps	Hinders
listening	talking
trying hard	being silly
I really want to do it	if people don't concentrate

Questions to prompt reflection

Reflecting on cooperative learning can be regularly encouraged through the questions teachers ask both during and after a cooperative learning activity. The following questions are designed to raise pupils' awareness of why they work this way, to raise the importance of each person's contribution and to improve their understanding of the processes involved.

- How well do you think your group worked today?
- How do you know you/your group worked well?
- What is one thing you saw someone do or heard someone say that helped the group work well?
- What is one thing that you saw someone do or heard someone say that made it hard for your group to work well together?
- How did you feel when you were working in your group?
- How do you know when a group is working well?
- What does a good group look like? Feel like? Sound like?
- What was one thing you think you did really well to help your group?
- What is something you would like to do better next time?
- Why do you think it is a good idea to work in groups?
- How is cooperative group work different to working by yourself?
- When do you like to work with others/alone? Why?
- What did you learn from working in a team?
- What is something you think you taught others in your group?
- What is something you learnt from others?
- What did you notice or learn about yourself?

Strategies to enhance reflection on cooperative learning

- Set or negotiate a specific focus or goal for the session. For example, 'As you work in your groups today, be aware of the contributions each pupil is making and how much time individuals take/get as you work together. At the end of the session, I will ask you to reflect on this as a group and we will talk about it together'. (See *Personal and Group Goals*, page 61 and *From Me to We*, page 63.)

- Pupils write a sentence about their experience in the group and then share that with others.

- Pupils write/talk about how they think another group member might have felt in their group and why.

- Pupils draw a picture of their group at a time when it was working well/poorly. Use speech balloons to show what the group members were saying. (See *Imagine You Are the Teacher*, page 64.)

- Design a reflection sheet (see pages 57–8) where the group must give themselves a score/smiley or sad face, etc for various aspects of their work.

- Two stars and a wish: groups identify two things they did well and one thing (a wish) they could do better next time.

Written and visual tasks

Class charts/criteria lists

Use class-made charts to assess progress. The focus could be identified by the teacher, the group or individuals. Not all groups need to be assessing the same foci.

Being thoughtful

✓	We looked at each other
	We gave 'pats on the back'
✓	We helped each other
	We encouraged others

Sharing

✓	tasks
✓	ideas
✓	jobs
	scissors

- Identify one or more aspects to observe across all groups, such as pupils encouraging each other.

- Focus on one or more groups during an allotted period of time, such as one week.

- Ask the pupils to focus on aspects from charts and self-assess. Groups can choose the aspects they need to work on.

- Ask pupils to select personal goals from class lists of criteria, and self-assess their performance in groups. (See the example opposite.)

THINKING ABOUT MY WORK

Name .... Activity .... Date ....

What I do	All the time	Some-times	I need to improve this	What could I do to improve my performance?
Listen to other people				
Allow people to participate equally			I'm trying but it's difficult. I dominate.	I should see if anyone has anything to say and then state my point of view.
Share resources and ideas				
Negotiate how to do things				
Cooperate with each other				
Am responsible for my role in the team				
Make good use of time				
Communicate positively with others				

Drawings or visual organisers

These could be used to demonstrate how pupils have worked as a group or how they have improved their team skills. The following example uses the 'Bridge' visual organiser.

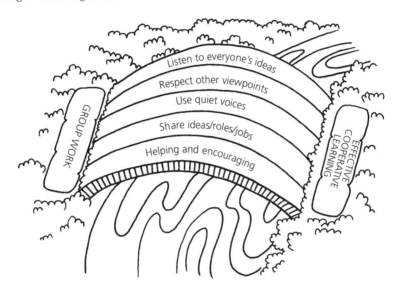

Performance or demonstrations

To cater for pupils who prefer to demonstrate their understandings in a kinesthetic mode, the following techniques could be used.

Freeze frame/human sculpture

The group must use their bodies to make a scene/model/structure to illustrate something. Everyone needs to participate. Add layers to this by asking that everyone touches at least one other person.

Fishbowl (see also page 13)

One group engages in the given task while other pupils (maybe another group or the whole class) observes the processes they use.

Observation, checklists and anecdotal notes

Use class charts or your own criteria to focus observation on individuals or groups. By keeping records of behaviour over time you should be able to track progress. Share these records with pupils.

Example of anecdotal notes

Name	Date	Understanding the problem	Selecting strategies	Collecting information	Patterns and options	Justifying/presenting	Task skills	Social skills	Work skills	Comments
			Problem Solving					Cooperative Learning		
Jamilla	24/4	✓	✓	✓	✓	✓	✓	✓	✓	Coordinating group tasks well
Lynette	28/4	✓			✓		✓		✓	Needs to listen to others' ideas
Kyle	1/5	✓	✓	✓				✓	✓	Capable but sometimes off task
Matthew	1/5	✓		✓		✓			✓	Discussed need for tolerance

Conferencing and discussions

By talking to, questioning and asking pupils about their questions we can collect valuable information about attitudes towards cooperative group skills. Conferencing and discussions can be conducted on a one-to-one, small group or whole class level.

Photographic records, tape recordings and video recordings

Use equipment to analyse pupil behaviour. This can be viewed by you and pupils a number of times. Review the images and comment on what they reveal about the way the group worked. For example, pupils can use digital photos to add captions, think bubbles, speech balloons or observations. A skills or criteria list could be used to record observations.

Reporting/using assessment and record keeping

Records can be used for a number of other purposes such as reporting to parents, teacher self-assessment and information for others. For example, photos can be used to produce class books for home loan and videos can be used for professional development and parent information nights.

A final note

In addition to these reporting purposes, assessment should be used to improve pupil learning. We encourage teachers to involve pupils in their own assessment as this can increase pupil responsibility for their own learning and utilise higher-order thinking.

Proformas for the classroom

Thank You Slips

Thank you ....
for helping others in your group.

Thank you ....
for listening so well to others.

Thank you ....
for speaking so clearly.

Thank you ....
for being kind to others.

Thank you ....
for sharing your ideas.

Thank you ....
for sharing materials.

Thank you ....
for staying focused.

Thank you ....
for letting someone else go first.

Thank You Slips

Thank you ....

for using friendly body language.

Thank you ....

for discussing various ideas.

Thank you ....

for presenting your ideas well to others.

Thank you ....

for effective problem solving.

Thank you ....

for thinking carefully about the group task.

Thank you ....

for taking a risk.

Thank you ....

Thank you ....

Reflect, Combine, Perform!

ON YOUR OWN

Think about the work you have done with your group. Finish the sentences in each box using only one or two words. When you have done this, cut out each strip.

I heard

I felt

I learnt

I am

AS A GROUP

Share your statements with each other and arrange them to make a group poem. You need to use all the statements – even if some are the same. You will need to perform your poem to the class so allow some time for practice!

Goal-based Assessment

Give yourself a sad or smiley face for each skill.

Skills	Team member 1	Team member 2	Team member 3	Team member 4	Team member 5
Accepting and providing constructive criticism					
Active listening					
Asking questions					
Checking and confirming					
Compromising					
Following directions					
Goal setting					
Justifying viewpoints					
Linking ideas					
Maintaining focus/ keeping on task					
Managing conflict or disagreement					
Managing time					
Negotiating					
Organising					
Planning					

Skills	Team member 1	Team member 2	Team member 3	Team member 4	Team member 5
Presenting ideas to others					
Problem solving					
Reflecting on learning, behaviour and thinking					
Reporting to others					
Risk taking					
Seeking clarification					
Self-assessment					
Sharing					
Suggesting alternatives					
Supporting or helping others					
Teaching others					
Understanding other points of view					
Using eye contact and appropriate body language					

Give yourself 3 stars for what your group did really well.

★ _____ ★ _____ ★ _____

Goals for next time	How will I achieve these goals?
• •	• •

Role Cards

Problem solver
Make suggestions about how to sort out problems if they arise

Go-for
Gather and return with necessary materials

Recorder
Record the group's ideas

Encourager
Encourage good ideas and acknowledge the people involved

Reporter
Report back to the class, teacher or another group

Observer
Watch and listen to the group – identify how they are working together, their strengths and weaknesses, and then report back to them or the class

Time keeper
Keep an eye on the clock and let the group know how long they have to go

Organiser/coordinator
Get the group going and help keep them on track

Using the Senses

Self	Peer

What I did to...
help someone else

What I saw...

be a good team member

What did I say...
that was encouraging

that was kind

How did I feel ...

Personal and Group Goals

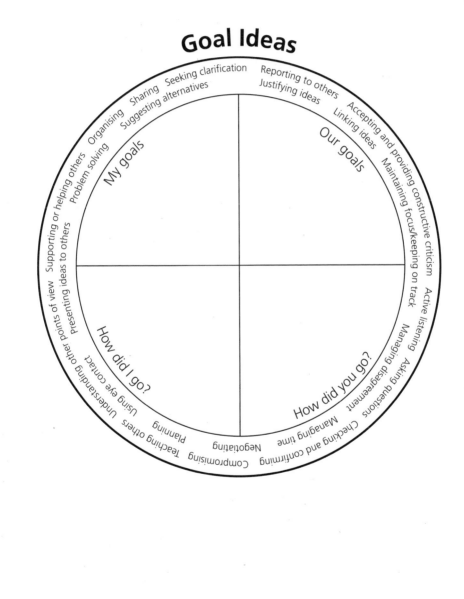

Goal Ideas

My goals
Organising · Sharing · Seeking clarification · Suggesting alternatives · Problem solving · Supporting or helping others

Our goals
Reporting to others · Justifying ideas · Accepting and providing constructive criticism · Linking ideas · Maintaining focus/keeping on track · Active listening · Asking questions · Managing disagreement · Managing time

How did I go?
Presenting ideas to others · Understanding other points of view · Using eye contact · Planning · Teaching others · Negotiating · Compromising

How did you go?
Checking and confirming

Cooperative Quiz

Tick whether you agree or disagree with the following statements.

Statement	Agree	Disagree
Cooperative work is like baking a good cake.		
When you work well with others you get more done.		
You don't have to use your brain when you work in cooperative groups.		
It's easier to work with others than to work alone.		
You need to use your body and brain to make cooperative group work effective.		
Boys and girls like to work differently in groups.		
It's important to listen more than you speak in cooperative groups.		
You have to be careful not to lose your temper in cooperative groups.		
One person always ends up doing more work than the others in cooperative groups.		
If you allocate roles, cooperative group work is a lot fairer.		
Most people prefer to work with others.		
It's easier to cooperate if you are working with good friends.		

Write a few of your own cooperative work statements.

_____

_____

_____

From Me to We

Individual thinking (my ideas)

_____

_____

_____

Group thinking (paired ideas)

What did you learn by working with a partner?

_____

_____

Did you change your mind about one of your ideas? If so, why?

_____

Imagine You Are the Teacher

If you were the teacher, what would you have seen while your group was working?
Draw this in the space below.

Add speech bubbles to your drawing.

If you were the teacher, what feedback would you have given to your group about:

1.   How well you worked

_____

_____

_____

2.   What you need to improve

_____

_____

_____

Further reading

Allard, A. and Wilson, J. (1995) *Gender Dimensions: Constructing interpersonal skills in the classroom*, Eleanor Curtain Publishing, South Yarra.

Bennett, B. and Rolheiser, C. (2001) *Beyond Manet: The artful science of instructional integration*, Bookation, Toronto.

Cornelius, H. and Faire, S. (1995) *Everyone Can Win: How to resolve conflict*, Simon Schuster, Brookvale, NSW.

Hill, S. and Hill, T. (1990) *The Collaborative Classroom: A guide to cooperative learning*, Eleanor Curtain Publishing, South Yarra.

Johnson, D. and Johnson, R. (1987) *Learning Together and Alone*, Prentice Hall, Englewood Cliffs, NJ.

Johnson, D. and Johnson, R. (1994) *Learning Together and Alone: Cooperative, competitive and individualistic learning*, Allyn and Bacon, Boston MA.

McGrath, H. and Francey, S. (1991) *Friendly Kids, Friendly Classrooms: Teaching social skills and confidence in the classroom*, Longman, Melbourne.

McGrath, H. and Francey, S. (1991) *Different Kids, Same Classroom*, Longman, Melbourne.

Murdoch, K. (1998) *Classroom Connections*, Eleanor Curtain Publishing, South Yarra.

Murdoch, K. and Wilson, J. (2004) *Learning Links*, Curriculum Corporation, Melbourne.

Reid, J. (2002) *Managing Small Group Learning*, PETA, Newtown, NSW.

Slavin, R. (1991) *Student Team Learning: A practical guide to cooperative learning* (3rd edn.), National Education Association, Washington, DC.

Townsend, J and Otero, G. (1999) *The Global Classroom*, Hawker Brownlow, Melbourne.